What's so special about Shakespeare?

PLAY

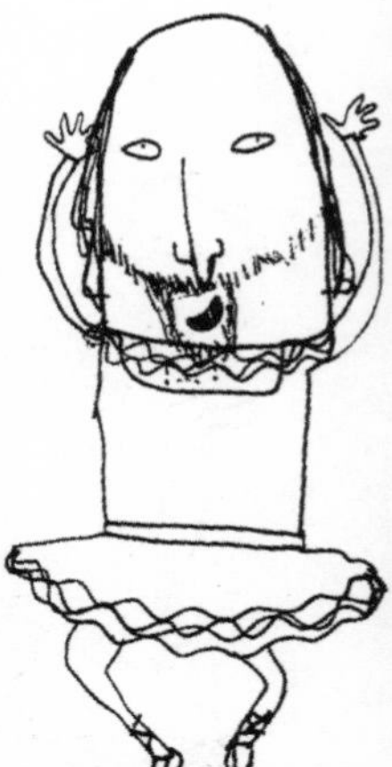

Wall

For Harold and Connie
who introduced me to Shaks.
M.R.

"Alas, poor Tim, he knows me well!"
S.N.

First published as *Shakespeare: His Work & His World* (2001)
by Walker Books Ltd, 87 Vauxhall Walk, London SE11 5HJ

This edition published 2016

4 6 8 10 9 7 5

The book has been typeset in ITC Usherwood

Printed and bound by CPI Group (UK) Ltd, Croydon, CR0 4YY

British Library Cataloguing in Publication Data:
a catalogue record for this book is
available from the British Library

978-1-4063-6741-6

www.walker.co.uk

What's so special about
Shakespeare?

MICHAEL ROSEN

illustrated by

SARAH NAYLER

WALKER
BOOKS

Liberty! Freedom!

Tyranny is dead!

Run hence, proclaim,

cry it about the streets.

***Julius Caesar**, Act 3, Scene 1*

Contents

A plot! 1598

It's the middle of the night on the edge of London, a few days after Christmas day, 1598. The River Thames is frozen over, snow is falling. The roofs of the timbered houses and the nearby fields are white with it. Four buildings stand higher than the nearby houses, shops, bowling-alleys, gambling houses and taverns – a windmill, a church and two theatres. One of the theatres is called the Curtain, and the other simply the Theatre. They are tall wooden buildings that have only been there for ten years or so but in that time their walls have shaken to the sound of swords clashing in fencing matches, actors crying of murder or lost love, and audiences roaring with laughter.

But tonight sixteen men are pulling down the Theatre. Two of them are brothers. They run a company of actors who put on plays, and with them there's a builder and his workmen.

As the men hurry about their work, it's clear that what's going on is secret and must be done as quickly as possible. Through the night the workmen load timbers onto wagons.

Two strangers arrive and start quizzing them. The workmen lie and say they are only taking down the parts of the building that are decaying. Really, they are dismantling the whole theatre and taking it somewhere else. It's a risky business because if it can be proved that they are stealing, they will all be hanged and their

severed heads put on show.

But before long the men are taking the timbers across London Bridge to Southwark, where the theatre will be rebuilt and become known as one of the world's most famous theatres: the Globe.

Those two theatres on the edge of London were where the first plays of William Shakespeare were put on. But Shakespeare wasn't the kind of writer who sent off his plays and sat around hoping someone might perform them. He was an actor who worked in the same company as those men who dismantled the Theatre, and what's more, he was one of the new owners of the Globe.

In the four hundred years since then, he has become one of the world's most famous writers.

A plot! 1598

What's so special about Shakespeare?

Watching Shakespeare's plays is like being invited into a house full of amazing rooms. Go through a door at the top of the house and you will meet a ghost walking the battlements of a castle at night. You will hear him telling a young man that he is the ghost of his father, the old king. What's more, the ghost reveals that he was murdered by his own brother. And then the ghost says:

> **If thou didst ever thy dear father love—**
> **Revenge his foul and most unnatural murder.**
> ***Hamlet,*** *Act 1, Scene 5*

What will the young man do?

Do I have to, Dad?
RIP

Walk into one of the rooms and you will come across a rich man yelling at his daughter because she won't marry the man he has chosen for her.

He shouts:

An* you be mine, I'll give you to my friend.
An you be not, hang, beg, starve, die in the streets...
Romeo and Juliet, *Act 3, Scene 5*

But the girl has secretly married another man.

What's going to happen?

***An** if

Move along into another room and a group of men are whispering amongst themselves. They are dressed in the clothes of Ancient Rome and they are working out how they are going to murder the future king:

> **And, gentle friends,**
> **Let's kill him boldly, but not wrathfully.**
> **Let's carve him as a dish fit for the gods,**
> **Not hew him as a carcass fit for hounds.**
> ***Julius Caesar**, Act 2, Scene 1*

Will they do it?

If they do, will they get away with it?

And out in the garden of the house, a bunch of crazy people have come up with a great practical joke. They've tricked a stuffy, mean-minded man into thinking that the sad, beautiful lady of the house has fallen in love with him. He is reading what he thinks is a love letter to him from the lady. He says:

> **...for every reason excites to this, that my lady loves me...**
> **I thank my stars, I am happy.**
> ***Twelfth Night**, Act 2, Scene 5*

But the letter's a forgery, written by the bunch of crazy people now watching him while he reads. What will happen next time the stuffy man meets the lady?

There are lots more amazing rooms, and if you go into them you will find trial scenes, battles, love potions, cruel kings, civil wars, assassinations, riots, witches, fairies, jesters, even a statue that comes to life. You will also meet people with deep and powerful emotions – wild jealousy, crazed hunger for power, terrible sadness, great happiness, sneering contempt.

All this may sound extraordinary, but Shakespeare lived in extraordinary times.

Extraordinary and dangerous times

So what was it like in England when Shakespeare was writing? These were dangerous times – even for a writer!

A few years earlier, one of the most famous playwrights of the day, Christopher Marlowe, had been stabbed to death during a fight. Another playwright, Ben Jonson, had killed someone and managed to get off with nothing more than having his left thumb branded, supposedly with a "T" for Tyburn – the place where he'd be executed if he was caught again. And, strange as it may seem, these were especially dangerous times if you were the king or queen.

Shakespeare lived under two monarchs: Elizabeth I and James I. Elizabeth was imprisoned in the Tower of London by her half-sister. Her father, Henry VIII, had her mother beheaded, and Elizabeth herself ordered the execution of her second cousin, Mary, Queen of Scots...

When James was king, Guy Fawkes and his friends tried to blow him up in the Houses of Parliament.

Shakespeare lived at a time when ordinary people didn't choose who ruled over them. Countries were ruled by someone who claimed that he (or, very rarely, she) had a right to rule because they belonged to a particular family. The people in this family would say there was a "royal line" that went back and back which proved that they were the "true" rulers. Many ordinary people looked up to these monarchs as if they were almost gods.

But in Britain several families claimed that they were the "true" rulers, and you have to remember that such families were rich enough to raise armies against each other. This meant that civil war – war between people in the same country – was always possible. Every year there was news of plots and rebellions.

There was also a big war with Spain, and bloody battles in Ireland and Holland.

Shakespeare wrote plays about the powerful families – the lords and dukes and princes – who wanted to rule England. In these plays, and in others set in Ancient Rome, we watch exciting scenes of civil wars, battles, rebellions, poor people's riots, conspiracies and wars between countries. And while all this is going on, the characters often discuss what makes a good ruler. What if your ruler were no good? Would it be right to get rid of him or her and put someone else in their place? Who should decide that? Should that be an argument left to the great families who had always ruled? Some of the people who thought they should have a say were people with no royal line but who had money and power. It was only thirty-three years after Shakespeare died that such people had the King's head chopped off and then chose a ruler, Oliver Cromwell, who had no royal line and who didn't even call himself a king!

In Shakespeare's time religion was much more important in people's lives than it is today. Nearly everyone in Britain described themselves as Christian but where there had once been only one Christian Church, there were now many. And wherever one kind of Christian gained power, they nearly always ended up trying to imprison or kill off the other kinds. All over Europe people were fighting huge bloody battles and civil wars against each other.

In England the trouble involved the ruling family, the Tudors. When the Tudor monarch was a Roman Catholic, Protestants were persecuted, arrested and sometimes burnt at the stake.

And when Elizabeth – a Protestant – came to the throne, it was extremely dangerous to be a Roman Catholic. Elizabeth had one hundred and twenty-three Catholic priests executed.

Protestants also fought each other. Some, nicknamed "Puritans" and "Quakers", were inventing a whole new way of life and preaching an end to high living, fun and games, gambling, sports, drinking, over-eating and street festivals.

Shakespeare came across these people not only as refugees from Holland but also

as the new rulers of the City of London, with the power to close theatres and ban plays. Small wonder we catch a glimpse of one or two unpleasant Puritans in his plays!

In some parts of Europe, Roman Catholics were in power; in others, Protestants. So the discussions over who should be king and what makes a good ruler were intertwined in Shakespeare's lifetime with questions about the right way to be a Christian.

Shakespeare lived amid all this political and religious talk. But it wasn't all talk. There was a lot of plotting and spying and murder going on as well. You often find people in his plays talking about the making and breaking of kings, as well as treachery and treason:

Peace, impudent and shameless Warwick,
peace!
Proud setter-up and puller-down of kings!
Henry VI Part *3, Act 3, Scene 3*

Shakespeare would have known that if you backed the wrong man, you could end up stabbed to death or executed. What's more, with the streets full of soldiers and ex-soldiers, there was always someone around who knew a lot about killing:

> **...when the searching eye of heaven is hid**
> **Behind the globe, that lights the lower world,**
> **Then thieves and robbers range abroad unseen**
> **In murders and in outrage bloody here...**
> ***Richard II**, Act 3, Scene 2*

But these dangerous times were also times of great change. Explorers were heading off all round the globe, discovering, among other things, that the earth was round and not flat.

The people of England and Europe now knew that there were many different countries in the world, and that vast amounts of money could be made if you came back to England with valuable cargoes.

Just after Shakespeare was born, John Hawkins found another way to make money: taking people from West Africa across the Atlantic Ocean and selling them in the Caribbean as slaves. In one of Shakespeare's plays we see a slave arguing for the right to live on his own land:

> **This island's mine, by Sycorax my mother,**
> **Which thou tak'st from me. When thou cam'st first,**
> **Thou strok'st me and made much of me, wouldst give me**
> **Water with berries in't...**
> ***The Tempest*, *Act 1, Scene 2***

And he goes on to complain:

> **...and here you sty me**
> **In this hard rock, whiles you do keep from me**
> **The rest o'th' island.**
> ***The Tempest**, Act 1, Scene 2*

We also see Shakespeare's characters realizing just how powerful money is. Two daughters turn against their own father because of their greed; a rich merchant nearly loses his life when he loses his money; and a nobleman despairs when he sees what evil things people will do for gold. He calls gold a yellow slave:

> **This yellow slave**
> **Will knit and break religions...**
> ***Timon of Athens**, Act 4, Scene 3*

Then he says it will turn thieves into lords and then politicians will approve of them.

Some other people in Shakespeare's time were discovering new plants and animals and bringing them back to Europe, studying languages, reading old books from Ancient Greece and Rome, and reading new books from Italy and France.

This desire to explore and discover was made easier by a revolution in how people communicated with each other. In England and Wales a hundred years earlier, most of the people who could read and write worked in the Church. Now, more and more people were getting an education. Many could read, even if they couldn't write. Jokes, stories, poetry, plays and ideas about politics were all appearing in print. You could find them written down in pamphlets, sometimes on single sheets of paper sold by ballad-sellers and, of course, in books.

All this meant that knowledge was no longer something that you had to remember.

It was something you could store on a page in a book in your pocket or in your house. And reading was not just for priests, bishops and the people close to the king. Someone like Shakespeare, from a tradesman's family living in a country town, could turn the knowledge he found in books into lines, scenes and whole plays. And what's more, he was not just an Englishman writing about things in England, but someone who took books, plays, poems and folk stories from Italy, Ancient Rome and from Arab countries, and turned them into dramas.

Sometimes Shakespeare changed the great words he found in old books and put them into the mouths of his characters, as he did with a description of Cleopatra floating down the river in a golden barge.

Here's part of the Roman book by someone called Plutarch, translated by Sir Thomas North and published in 1579:

> **...she disdained to set forward otherwise,**
> **but to take her barge in the river of Cydnus, the**
> **poop whereof was gold, the sails of purple, and**
> **the oars of silver, which kept stroke in**
> **rowing**
> **after the sound of the music of flutes,**
> **oboes, citherns, viols,**
> **and such other instruments**
> **as they played upon in the barge.**

Here's the Shakespeare, written in 1606–7:

> **The barge she sat in, like a burnished throne**
> **Burned on the water. The poop was beaten gold;**
> **Purple the sails, and so perfumèd that**
> **The winds were love-sick with them. The oars were silver,**
> **Which to the tune of flutes kept stroke, and made**
> **The water which they beat to follow faster,**
> **As amorous of their strokes.**
> *Antony and Cleopatra*, Act 2, Scene 2

So it wasn't just that Shakespeare lived through extraordinary times – what's fascinating is that his plays show this in so many different ways. His characters are always plotting and scheming, coming up with ideas for doing something new and clever. There are noblemen trying to get rid of the king, a duke disguising himself in order to find out what's really going on in his country, and a ruler who thinks he's been wronged planning his revenge. And in the dramatic climaxes and endings of the plays, we see people having to face the consequences of the things they have said and done. We see the tragedy of the king who spurned the one daughter who really loved him – they both die; and the tragedy of the soldier who believed the lies of the man he thought was his friend rather than the true words of his wife – the soldier and his wife die.

In the stories and scenes of Shakespeare's plays, we have a sense of the extraordinary and dangerous things that could and did happen during his lifetime.

Shakespeare: the facts

Where did this amazing writer come from? How did he spend his childhood? What did he do when he was a young man? Did he live until old age?

If a writer like Shakespeare had lived a hundred years ago, there would be many ways of finding out the answers to these questions: he might have left a diary, there would be people's memories of him written down, letters from him and to him, newspaper articles, books about him by people who knew him and so on. But in the records of Shakespeare's time, we only find such writing when it's about important people like the queen.

We don't even know the exact day William Shakespeare was born! All we know is that he was christened in the Holy Trinity Church of Stratford-upon-Avon in Warwickshire on 26 April 1564. We know that his mother came from a well-off farming family, and that at the time of his birth, Shakespeare's father was doing well in business, making and selling leather gloves, purses, belts, aprons and fleeces.

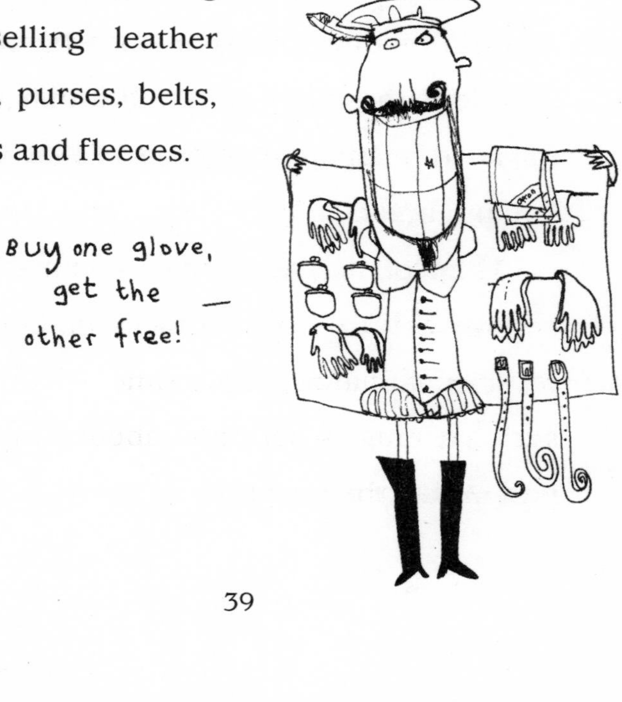
Buy one glove, get the other free!

And we know that William was the third of eight children: Joan and Margaret, who both died young; then William himself; and then Gilbert; a second Joan; Anne (who died when she was seven); Richard; and finally, Edmund. The next time we hear about Shakespeare, it's 1582. He's eighteen and getting married to someone called Anne Hathaway, who is eight years older than him and is already expecting their first baby. Six months later a girl called Susanna is born, followed nearly two years after that by twins – Judith and Hamnet.

Then once again we know nothing for certain until ten years later, when Shakespeare is twenty-eight in 1592. We find out that one of his plays, *Henry VI, Part 1*, is being put on in London at the Rose Theatre, not far from what is now Southwark Cathedral.

A few months later a rival playwright called Robert Greene (whose plays weren't very popular) dies. He leaves behind a piece of writing called *Greene's Groatsworth of Wit* in which he calls Shakespeare "an upstart crow, beautified with our feathers" and a "*Johannes fac totum*"– that's Latin for a Jack of all trades.

I'm so popular.
There's no need to crow about it, Will.

He also says that Shakespeare thought of himself as "the only Shake-scene in a country". It sounds a bit like an older pop star moaning about a younger one for stealing his way of singing, playing too many instruments and being vain! Between the ages of twenty-eight and thirty-two we know that Shakespeare was writing poetry and plays, and that he was acting in a company called the Lord Chamberlain's Men. When he was thirty-two we know that his son Hamnet died, and that he was in trouble with the law and had to promise to keep the peace.

In 1597, Shakespeare had earned enough money to buy one of the biggest houses back in his home town of Stratford. The following year he was in trouble with the law again, this time for what's known as "hoarding".

He kept a big store of corn and ale because he hoped that the price would go up and he could sell it at a profit. And yet in his play *Coriolanus*, the poor rebel against people who did this:

> **...their store-houses crammed with grain;**
> **make edicts* for usury to support usurers...***
> ***Coriolanus**, Act 1, Scene 1*

***edicts** laws
***usury** making profit from lending money

It was at the end of 1598 that Shakespeare and his friends were involved in the escapade that opens this book: moving a theatre from Shoreditch across London Bridge to Southwark. They did this because their landlord wanted more and more rent, and he was so angry about it that he took them to court. The landlord lost the case because he was only entitled to have rent off

Get the hint, you lot?
ouch!

them for the land. He didn't own the wood of the theatre itself. They got away with it!

The following year saw the building of the Globe Theatre, using some of the timbers from the old theatre in Shoreditch. Shakespeare owned one-tenth of it. In 1601, we know that Shakespeare's company accepted a bribe from supporters of the Earl of Essex who was leading a rebellion against the Queen. Essex asked them to put on a play, *Richard II*, that showed a weak king being removed from the throne.

A few days later, the Earl of Essex was caught and beheaded. It would have been a dangerous time for Shakespeare and his friends.

In 1602, we know that Shakespeare's play *Twelfth Night* was put on in a hall that is still standing today, the Middle Temple in London. He bought more land and a cottage in Stratford and in 1603, now that King James had come to the throne, his theatre company became known as the King's Men. It was a kind of promotion to being the top theatricals of the day. Now many of Shakespeare's plays were being put on at the court.

In 1607, Shakespeare's daughter Susanna married a doctor, John Hall, and his brother Edmund died. His brother Gilbert died in 1612, and his brother Richard a year later, which meant that William was now the only male Shakespeare alive in his family. In the same year, 1613, he bought some property in Black-friars and the Globe Theatre burnt down.

He became involved in yet more legal problems in 1615, this time over whether a landowner had the right to put fences round land that everyone used for grazing animals. It seems that the people on Stratford town council were against the landowners but Shakespeare wouldn't join either side in the argument.

In 1616, Shakespeare wrote and rewrote his will, and died at the age of fifty-two.

So do we have to leave it at that? Is that all we can say about him? No, because we can build up a picture of what life was like for someone like Shakespeare who grew up in Stratford at this time, who went to one of the most exciting cities in the world, someone who was doing the big new thing – putting on plays.

Stratford and school

These days we would think Shakespeare's Stratford was very small. There weren't many more than a thousand people living there.

They lived in what are called half-timbered houses and cottages. But it was a market town, which meant that people from the nearby villages came there to sell their cattle and whatever they had harvested. It was also a crossroads between places to the west, like Wales, and places to the south, like London, and this made it a busy town.

Around and about Stratford were woods, hills, streams, fields and farms. Shakespeare's plays are full of such places, where we can perhaps imagine he spent many hours of spare time.

If Shakespeare went to school, which seems very likely, then he would have gone to the King's New School in Stratford, maybe starting at the age of five. He would have gone six days a week, every week of the year, except for holy days like Easter and Christmas. The school day ran from six in the morning to six in the evening, beginning and ending with prayers. There was a two-hour lunch break.

In his play *As You Like It*, Shakespeare writes of the "whining" schoolboy:

> **...with his satchel**
> **And shining morning face, creeping like snail**
> **Unwillingly to school.**
> ***As You Like It*, *Act 2, Scene 7***

He would have learnt to read from a

kind of board called a hornbook. On it were the letters of the alphabet, sometimes in the shape of a cross, and the Lord's Prayer. Shakespeare mentions this in another play:

> **Monsieur, are you not lettered?**
> **Yes, yes, he teaches boys the horn-book.**
> ***Love's Labour's Lost,*** *Act 5, Scene 1*

He would have learnt prayers, and question and answer pieces called the

catechism. Then when he was seven he would have moved on to learning Latin. He would have come across Aesop's *Fables* and some Roman comedies by people like Plautus. Later, he would have read many more Latin poems and stories. Bits and pieces from them, and sometimes whole storylines, crop up in his plays.

The other book that Shakespeare would have known inside out was the Bible. We can tell which stories struck a chord with him. The story of Cain, who kills his brother Abel, is mentioned in the plays more than twenty-five times!

By the time Shakespeare was thirteen, his father's business was going downhill. It is only guesswork, but he may have had to leave school at this time because his father could not pay for him to stay there. Some people think that Shakespeare became a butcher's boy! This is because in his plays he seems to know so much about the trade of butchering meat. Others think he may have started training or done time as a lawyer, a doctor, a sailor, a falconer or a gardener, because the plays seem to show so much knowledge of these professions too. Of course, he may just have worked in his father's business, making and selling leather goods.

But let's face it, we don't really know very much about how Shakespeare spent his childhood and teenage years. We know what he *might* have thought about growing up, though, from the words of an old shepherd in one of his plays:

I would there were no age between ten and three-and-twenty, or that youth would sleep
out the rest;
for there is nothing in the between but getting wenches
with child, wronging the ancientry, stealing,
fighting...
***The Winter's Tale**, Act 3, Scene 3*

In other words, teenage pregnancy, being rude to old people, and stealing and fighting. What's new!

Shakespeare himself was a teenage father, and we don't catch another glimpse of him till he's twenty-eight years old and living in London.

London

Another way in which we can find out something about Shakespeare is by looking at the city where he spent so much of his life.

Greater London today has almost 10 million people living in it. In Shakespeare's time only two hundred thousand people were living there. Most of them had been born in England and Scotland but about five thousand had come from other countries – there were religious wars going on in and around Holland, and many were Puritan refugees.

Even though Tudor London might seem small by today's standards, it was seen in its time to be a huge, bustling, important place, "too much pestered with people" as the historian John Stow wrote, many living in "multitudes of base tenements". Right through the middle of the city ran the River Thames. It was packed with boats, and its three miles of quayside were busy with people loading and unloading goods from all over Britain, Europe and newly explored parts of the world. "Most of the inhabitants are employed in buying and selling merchandise, and trading in almost every corner of the world," said the Duke of Wurtemberg, who was visiting London in 1592.

All walks of life could be found in London. There was the court with its various palaces, where Queen Elizabeth I and then King James I lived, surrounded by hundreds of advisers, servants, entertainers and hangers-on.

There were the very rich who were setting up new banking and money-lending businesses. Such people might have owned two houses – a big country house just outside London and a grand town house.

There were the merchants who got together in groups called liveries and through their line of business – wool, gold,

manufacture or whatever – had a big say in how London and England were run.

There were thousands of tradesmen and shopkeepers living and working in small buildings or on stalls in the markets. There were the people who worked for all these others – the labourers and journeymen, as they were often called. And there were the out-of-work poor – the unemployed soldiers, old people, beggars and street people.

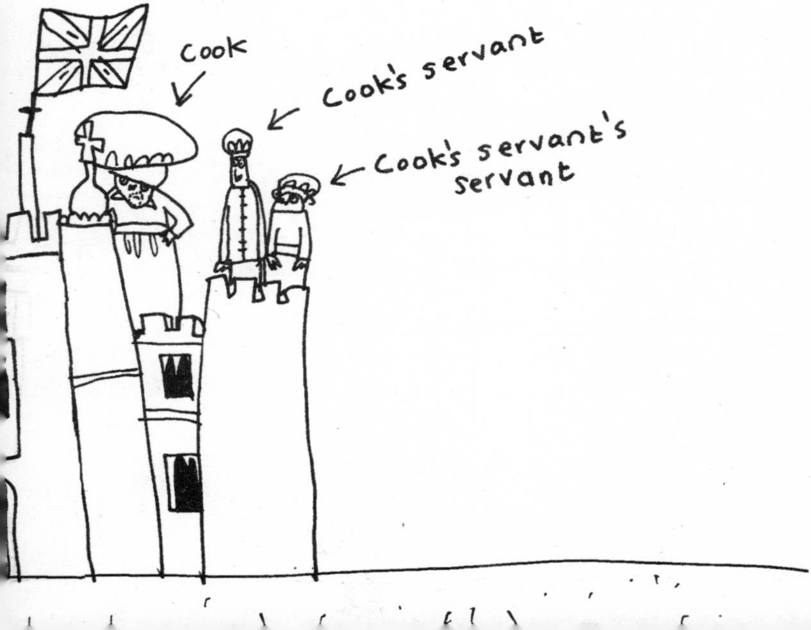

In and amongst them all, thousands of people such as bishops, priests, nuns and friars lived and worked in the Church.

In Shakespeare's plays, we meet the people of London. Within sight of the whole city stood the Tower, a place of dreadful executions and plots, and in *Hamlet* we find a prince walking the battlements of a castle full of murder and rumours of murder:

> **My father's spirit in arms! All is not well.**
> **I doubt some foul play. Would the night were come.**
> **Till then, sit still, my soul. Foul deeds will rise,**
> **Though all the earth o'erwhelm them, to men's eyes.**
> ***Hamlet**, Act 1, Scene 2*

In *The Merchant of Venice*, Antonio, a rich merchant, wheels and deals with a money-lender.

Thou know'st that all my fortunes are at sea,
Neither have I money nor commodity.*
To raise a present sum.*
***The Merchant of Venice**, Act 1, Scene 1*

In *Henry IV, Part 2* a gang of ruffians are called up to fight in the army. In *Romeo and Juliet*, Juliet rushes to a friar to find a way to marry her lover in secret. In *The Winter's Tale*, Autolycus sells ballads and stories.

In *Hamlet*, the king hires spies and hitmen just as Queen Elizabeth and her advisers hired people to do the same sort of job. And in *Coriolanus*, people riot over high prices, just as they did in London in Shakespeare's time.

We meet gravediggers, lawyers, school-teachers, servants and many, many more. We hear from people who want to kill their

***commodity** valuable goods
***present sum** a sum of ready money

king and we meet angry crowds of poor people. Like London itself, Shakespeare's plays teem with life.

Theatre in the making

As you look across the centuries, the kinds of entertainment that people enjoy change. Once there was no such thing as a film, then in the space of a few years millions of people all over the world were going to cinemas and watching them. But though they came quickly, films did not come out of nowhere: they were, in part, based on other kinds of entertainment that were already around, like plays and music hall shows.

It was a bit like that with the Elizabethan theatre Shakespeare found himself working in. When he was a boy, nearly everyone would have known about two kinds of popular show.

Mummers' plays were put on by local

people at festival times and tell the story of St George, who is killed and then magically rises up, usually cured by a crazy doctor. The characters speak in rhymes, they sing songs, and there's room for a few local jokes. These plays could be put on anywhere: in town squares, barns or fields. There are parts of Britain where they're still performed, sometimes in schools, and there's a special pleasure in thinking that Shakespeare, living as he did in the countryside, would certainly have known about mummers' plays.

Another kind of popular show was the mystery play – sometimes called the miracle play. Nowadays we all know about the Nativity play, written and rewritten by ordinary people and acted out by anyone of any age. In Shakespeare's time, people used to write and act out many more of the stories from the Bible. In some of these we find invented scenes, like an argument between Noah and his wife, or a man who steals a sheep from one of the shepherds in the Nativity play. Shakespeare is probably mentioning these mystery plays when Hamlet talks of an actor who overacts as one who "out-Herods Herod," Herod being the king in Palestine when Jesus was born.

People also acted out versions of old plays and stories that weren't from the Bible – we see this in *A Midsummer Night's Dream* when a group of workmen stage a play called "Pyramus and Thisbe" about two lovers who die.

Yet another kind of play – the morality

play – started appearing about a hundred years before Shakespeare's birth. This was a religious entertainment in which the characters had names like Charity and Folly and argued amongst themselves about the best way to behave.

As well as all these different kinds of theatre, nearly everyone would at some time in their lives have seen big public pageants and processions, rather like the ones we see today, with dances and mimes enacted and re-enacted as part of the procession. Kings, queens, dukes and lords were fond of all these entertainments which they put on in public or in their palaces and mansions. They also enjoyed shows called masques – a kind of fancy dress dance, often with songs and a magical theme. We come across them in Shakespeare's plays, and we know that Queen Elizabeth's father, Henry VIII, took part in an Italian-style

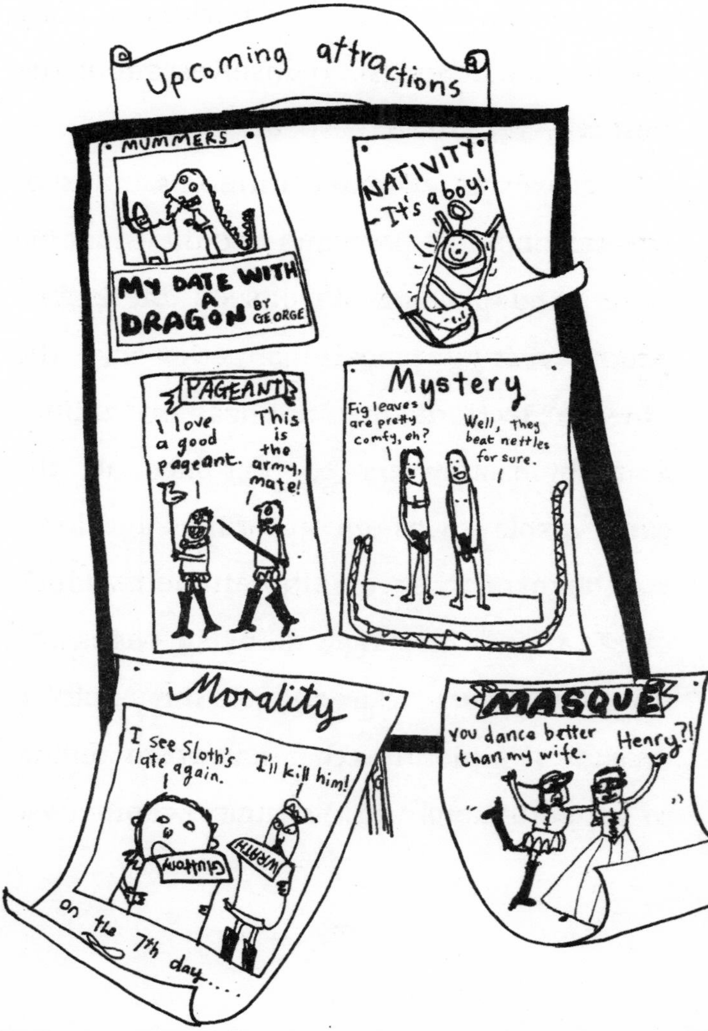

masque, dressed up in gold garments. He and the other masquers were hidden under "visors and caps of gold" and after the banquet was done they "came in ... and desired the ladies to dance." There is every chance young Shakespeare would have seen a variety of entertainments: a royal procession, local pageants and plays put on by touring players. We know that in his youth, visiting players came twenty-five times to Stratford and that Elizabeth I visited a nearby castle where a great pageant with water displays was put on for her.

Shakespeare's childhood and youth mark a time in England when teams of travelling players toured the country putting on shows. Sometimes they had a rich person to support them and then they were called things like Lord Strange's Men or the Lord Chamberlain's Men. Shakespeare himself joined a group of players, first as an actor and then as a resident playwright. The fact that these travelling players were doing all this work made possible the huge revolution in playwriting and theatre that took place in Shakespeare's time.

Theatre was becoming more popular and more groups of travelling players were getting together. They all needed plays to act and places to act in. When they first worked, they had no theatres. Sometimes they put on shows for the rich in big rooms and halls around the country. But when they performed in the courtyards of inns, they reached a much wider audience. We know that inns in London were being used for plays from just before Shakespeare's birth and by the time he came to London and joined the Lord Chamberlain's Men, the first theatres had just been built. It was a good time to be in showbiz. For the first time, actors were making enough money to build and own theatres.

And something else was happening. Some of the cleverest minds alive were writing plays full of action, tension and fully fledged characters. Young Christopher Marlowe wrote a play called *Tamburlaine the Great* about an incredibly violent king. Clever people with an education, like Ben Jonson, were writing plays full of wit and learning. It was just like the birth of the film industry or TV: new companies, a new way of putting on shows and a desperate need for new scripts.

Throughout Shakespeare's life, new playwrights were appearing, hundreds of new plays were being written and theatres were popping up all round the edges of the City of London.

The new theatres

These theatres had a special shape. If you go to the Globe Theatre in London or other similar theatres in the USA, Canada, Japan and New Zealand, you can see what they looked like.

The buildings were round or octagonal with an open-air space in the middle and

covered galleries round the edges. The stage was at one side and stuck out into the audience. When Juliet appears at her window dreaming of Romeo, she would have been on a balcony above the stage, while the ghost in *Macbeth* would probably have come up through a trapdoor in the floor. There were no curtains across the front of the stage, so the beginnings and

ends of scenes were just marked by the actors coming on and off. There were no elaborate stage paintings or sets either, and that's why, over and over again, we hear the characters in Shakespeare's plays saying where they are and what they can see:

> **But look, the morn in russet mantle* clad**
> **Walks o'er* the dew of yon* high eastern hill.**
> ***Hamlet**, Act 1, Scene 1*

In the introductions and end pieces to his plays Shakespeare often asks the audience to think about the imagination that's needed to enjoy a play:

> **Think, when we talk of horses, that you see them,**
> **Printing their proud hoofs i'th'* receiving earth...**
> *Henry V, Prologue*

***russet mantle** red coat
***o'er** over
***yon** that
***i'th'** in the

Because there were no theatre lights, the characters often have to say what time of day it is:

> **How sweet the moonlight sleeps upon this bank!**
> *The Merchant of Venice, Act 5, Scene 1*

No women ever acted in plays, so their parts were taken by boys.

This may be why we find such vivid descriptions of women:

> **O, she doth teach the torches to burn bright!**
> **It seems she hangs upon the cheek of night**
> **As a rich jewel in an Ethiope's ear –**
> **Beauty too rich for use, for earth too dear.**
> *Romeo and Juliet, Act 1, Scenes*

Some of the audience watched the play from the stage itself, some stood in front of the stage looking up at it, while the rest sat in rows all round. A Swiss visitor called Thomas Platter described these audiences in 1599:

> **...anyone who remains on the level standing pays only one English penny: but if he wants to sit, he is let in at a further door, and there he gives another penny. If he desires to sit on a cushion in the most comfortable place of all, where he not only sees everything well, but can also be seen, then he gives yet another English penny at another door.**

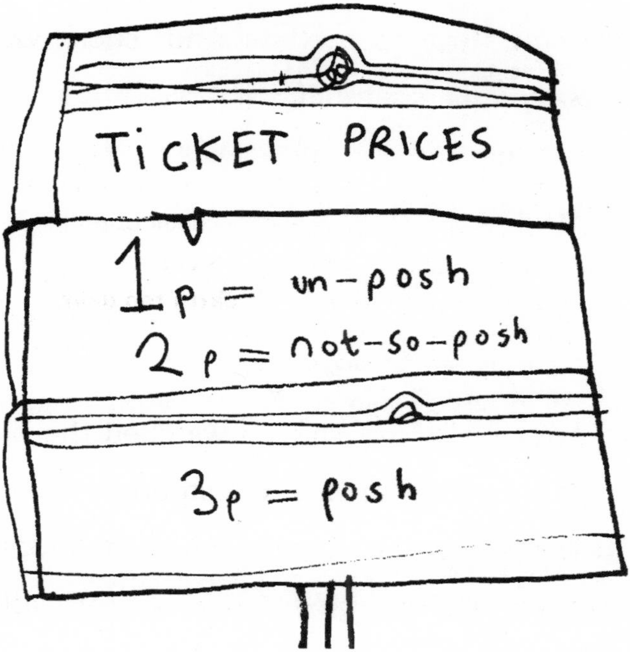

While the plays were on, some people talked, shouted, ate, drank and heckled. One of Shakespeare's characters says:

> **These are the youths that thunder at a playhouse, and fight for bitten apples...**
> ***Henry VIII**, Act 5, Scene 3*

The Puritans in their churches and in their council chambers weren't happy. They didn't like the way plays led to "frays and quarrels" and tried to ban them:

> **Satan hath not a more speedy way, fitter school to work and teach his desire to bring men and women into his snare of concupiscence and filthy lusts of whoredom, than those places and plays…**

This is a way of saying that theatres tempted people into all kinds of sin: overeating, drunkenness and the wrong kind of sex.

The Puritans kept trying to close the theatres, and they had to be closed again and again because of the plague, which killed over a fifth of the population of London at the time. But though it wasn't always easy to put on plays, nothing could stop the growing popularity of the theatre. By 1604, Shakespeare and his company were well on the way to becoming national celebrities.

Shakespeare at work

People argue about exactly how many plays Shakespeare wrote because he shared the writing of a few of them and others have been lost. That's why it's best to say that he probably wrote thirty-five plays and had a hand in writing another six or so. We know when many of them were first performed and put on the official register. This doesn't tell us exactly when they were written but it gives us a sense of them rolling out, one after another, for more than twenty years.

They are an incredible set of stories, full of action, poetry, tension, love, death, fun, music, dance, war, rebellion, conspiracy, betrayal and more. Sometimes they are about politics, at other times about how people get on together as man and woman, parent and child, friend and friend.

You don't have to divide the plays up into groups but ever since they were first put together in a book, people have done this. So, for example, plays that are about English history are usually called the history plays.

History
Now is the winter of our discontent...
Richard III

Plays that show a kind of flaw in a person's character which leads them into wicked or mistaken ways are usually called tragedies.

Tragedy

Hubble bubble, toil and trouble ...

Macbeth

Shakespeare wrote several set in Ancient Rome, so these are often called the Roman plays.

Roman
Let not a traitor live!
Julius Caesar

Plays that show the crazy and absurd things people get up to are called comedies,

Comedy
This is to make an ass of me.
A Midsummer Night's Dream

and others, which are like long folk stories, are sometimes called the romances.

Romance
I'll make you
the queen of Naples!
The Tempest

And there are one or two plays that don't seem to fit any of these groups, so they are called the problem plays, though the only people they seem to cause a problem for are the ones coming up with all these names!

When you have been to a few Shakespeare plays, you start seeing how a Roman play might also be called a tragedy, or how a romance is a kind of comedy. In fact, if you want to make up your own groups, you can. You could call some of them war plays, love plays and so on.

Most people first come across Shakespeare at school, when teachers try very hard to choose a play or part of a play that they think will interest young people. Their favourites for this are *A Midsummer Night's Dream*, *Macbeth*, *Romeo and Juliet*, *Henry IV, Part 1*, *Julius Caesar*, *King Lear*, *The Merchant of Venice*, *Measure for Measure*, *Twelfth Night* and *The Tempest*. These are all very different plays to see or read, and we're going to look more closely at four of them.

A Midsummer Night's Dream

In the comedy *A Midsummer Night's Dream*, Shakespeare moves very quickly between three groups of characters: lords and ladies; workmen; and fairies. The lords and ladies tie themselves into all kinds of knots over who loves whom, though some of this is the fairies' fault for throwing magic love potion in the wrong people's eyes. The workmen get into a knot trying to put on a play to show to the lords and ladies. Part of the

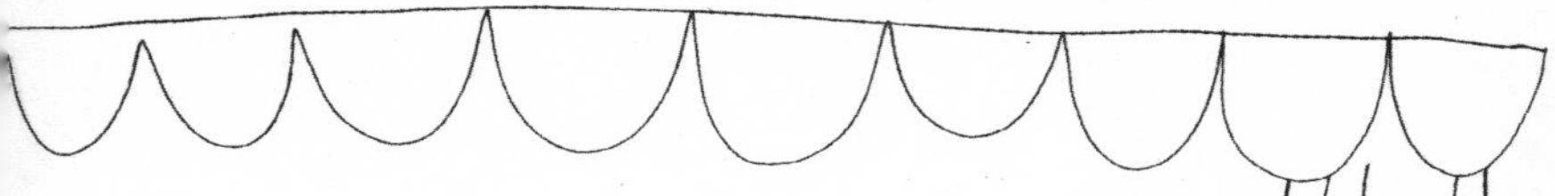

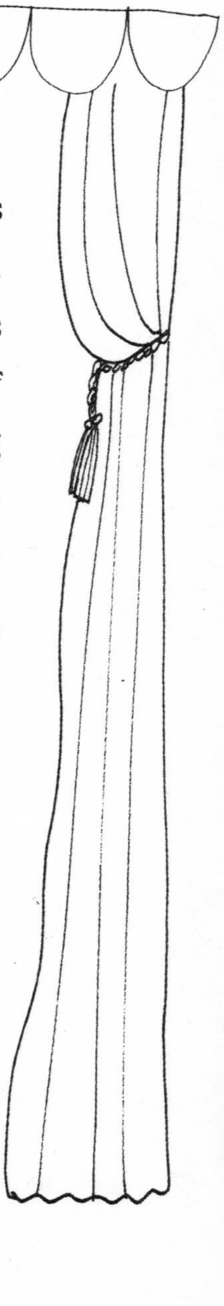

problem for them is that the fairies stick an ass's head on one of them. Meanwhile, the fairies themselves are in yet another knot because of the great jealousy between their king and queen. And again, part of the problem is the games the fairies play with that magic love potion. The king of the fairies uses it to make his queen fall in love with the workman wearing the ass's head.

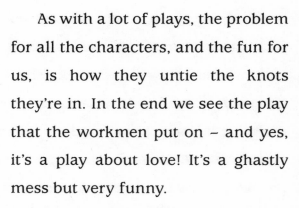

As with a lot of plays, the problem for all the characters, and the fun for us, is how they untie the knots they're in. In the end we see the play that the workmen put on – and yes, it's a play about love! It's a ghastly mess but very funny.

What makes all this so much more than a bit of supernatural fun is that what each of the three groups gets up to is a kind of comment on the others. So while the lords and ladies find themselves tormented by who loves whom, the workmen are putting on a play about a love affair that goes wrong and the fairy king and queen are in a fierce lovers' quarrel. Instead of seeing love as if it were just one colour, we see it in many different colours: its craziness, its sadness, its jealous side and even its dangerous side.

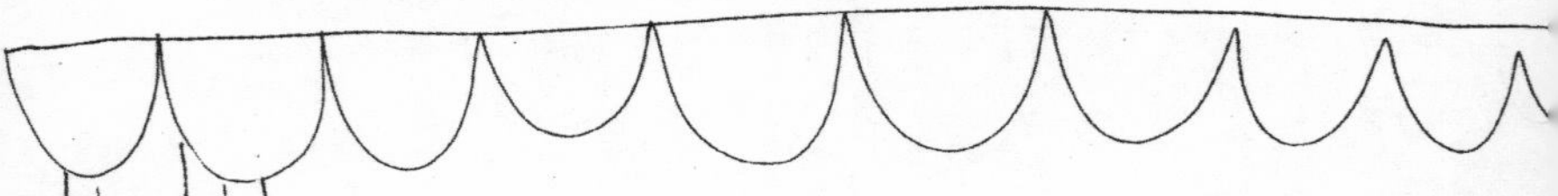

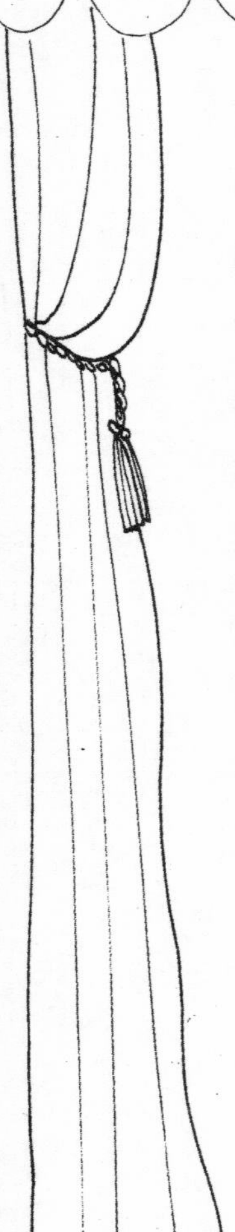

Macbeth

In the tragedy *Macbeth* we have a very different Shakespeare. It is a play in which he is asking questions about what makes a good ruler. Macbeth, a Scottish lord, is so desperately keen to be king that he murders everyone who stands in his way. He doesn't do this on his own,

however. First, three witches tell him that he will become king, giving him a motive. Later, we see how he is egged on by his wife, Lady Macbeth. The play is short, fast-moving and full of action, but even so, Shakespeare takes us deep into Macbeth's mind.

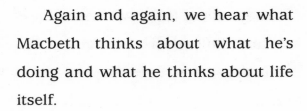

Again and again, we hear what Macbeth thinks about what he's doing and what he thinks about life itself.

It's interesting to wonder what effect this might have had on audiences in Shakespeare's time. After all, when the play was written, many people still thought that kings and queens were like gods. What happens if they're also criminals? Is it right to raise an army and fight them? Even though the play rushes on, we have time to hear what the people of Macbeth's country think of him.

They talk of how suspicious they are and how they see the whole country being ruined. We hear one lord say:

Alas, poor country,
Almost afraid to know itself…
Where sighs and groans and shrieks that rend the air
Are made, not marked…*
Act 4, Scene 3

So, as we saw with *A Midsummer Night's Dream*, we are not left with one view of a character or an event, but have a chance to see what one group of people thinks of another.

***marked** noticed

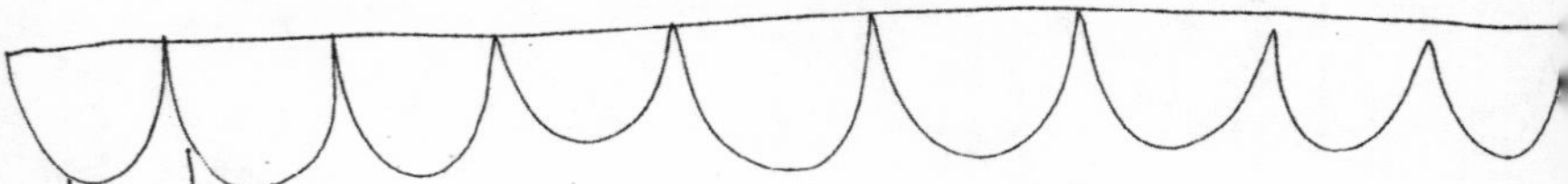

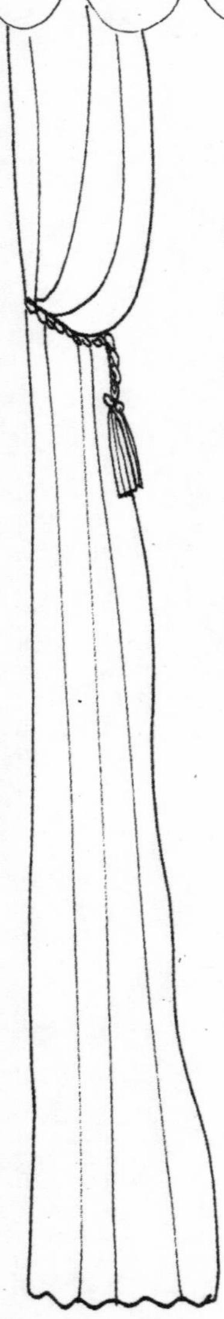

King Lear

In another tragedy, *King Lear,* we see a country falling apart. The play begins with Lear dividing his kingdom into three, and saying that whichever of his three daughters loves him the most will get the biggest portion. Goneril and Regan tell him they love him more

than words can say, but Lear's favourite, Cordelia, will not play along with this flattery. She says she loves her father, but has nothing more to add. Lear is enraged and says:

> **Nothing can come of nothing.**
> *Act 1, Scene 1*

He disowns Cordelia, and gives the kingdom over to his other two daughters. This means that he has to rely on them to look after him.

The play also tells a second story about the Earl of Gloucester, who has two sons, Edgar and Edmund. Like Lear, Gloucester rejects the good child (Edgar) in favour of the bad one (Edmund). In the play, the older generation discover that they have children who do not care for them and who plot against them. Goneril and Regan turn Lear out of their houses, even though they had said they loved him. Sadly, the two fathers reject the children who truly love them and they both end up broken and destroyed. Gloucester is blinded, and Lear goes mad.

Some of the most memorable scenes in Shakespeare's writing take place on a heath at night, where Lear and his jester face up to the elements:

> **Blow, wind, and crack your cheeks!**
> **Rage, blow,**
> **You cataracts and hurricanoes, spout**
> **Till you have drenched the steeples...**
> *Act 3, Scene 2*

In a little hut on the heath, Lear discovers how hard life is for poor people and calls on the rich to share their wealth. When Lear becomes mad, he starts to talk a strange kind of sense. In complicated sentences, he says how he now sees the world:

> **Plate sin with gold,**
> **And the strong lance of justice hurtless breaks;**
> **Arm it in rags, a pygmy's straw does pierce it.**
> *Act 4, Scene 5*

In other words, if rich people sin, no law or judge is strong enough to punish them. If poor people do bad things, they are too weak to escape punishment.

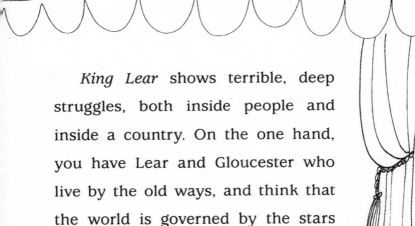

King Lear shows terrible, deep struggles, both inside people and inside a country. On the one hand, you have Lear and Gloucester who live by the old ways, and think that the world is governed by the stars and planets. On the other hand, you have the younger generation, Edmund, Goneril and Regan, who say things like:

> **Let me, if not by birth, have lands by wit.**
> *Act 1, Scene 2*

In other words: I'll get lands using my

own intelligence, as I can't have them by being born a nobleman.

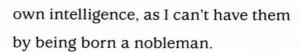

Shakespeare seems to be talking about a new kind of person appearing in England, who said that you didn't need a royal or noble name to get rich. He shows this new kind of person as ruthless, greedy and vicious, and the result of their behaviour as mutiny, treason and "the bond cracked 'twixt son and father."

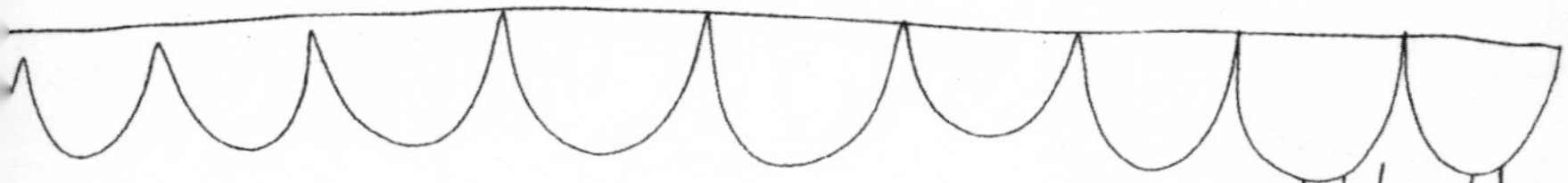

This kind of talk must have seemed very topical to Shakespeare's audiences at the Globe who lived in times of such great change.

The Tempest

This is a romance – one of the plays that's like a long folk tale. Most of the action takes place on an island, where a magician called Prospero rules. He was once a duke but was thrown out of power by his brother. On the island live Prospero's daughter, Miranda; his faithful fairy slave, Ariel; and his rebellious slave, Caliban. When a ship sails nearby carrying his brother, the king, and various followers and servants, Prospero conjures up a storm which shipwrecks them on the island.

Prospero's main ambition is to punish his brother and get his dukedom back. So the action of the play turns on just how much Prospero can control. He seems to have power over the elements; he contrives to make the king's son fall in love with his daughter; he watches while people plot each other's death, but intervenes before anything happens; and then he heads off a revolt when two of the shipwrecked sailors team up with his slave, Caliban.

Much of the play is about who's in charge, who's entitled to be in charge and what happens when the people who are ruled over don't like it. For instance, Prospero makes the king's son, Ferdinand, his slave for a while, and another character dreams of a society where everyone is free and equal.

At the very moment when we have learnt how badly people can behave, Prospero's daughter, Miranda, sets eyes on the first human beings she has seen apart from her father and Ferdinand and says, "O brave new world that has such people in't..." Sometimes the audience laugh when they hear her say that, and it's one of many examples of what's called dramatic irony in Shakespeare's plays. He makes us think about what we have just seen because we know that in some way or another the character who is speaking has got it wrong.

Though Shakespeare wasn't the first playwright to write plays full of irony, he was, and still is, one of the writers to do it most powerfully and skilfully. You may hear people say this or that is ironic – that's partly because Shakespeare put irony on the stage in so many dramatic ways.

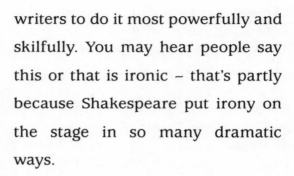

It so happens that *The Tempest* is one of his last plays, and in it there is a speech by Prospero that sounds to many people like Shakespeare himself signing off from creating all the stage magic of the previous twenty years and more…

Our revels now are ended. These our actors,
As I foretold you, were all spirits, and
Are melted into air, into thin air;
And like the baseless fabric of this vision,
The cloud-capped towers, the gorgeous palaces,
The solemn temples, the great globe itself,
Yea, all which it inherit, shall dissolve;
And, like this insubstantial pageant faded,
Leave not a rack behind. We are such stuff
As dreams are made on, and our little life
Is rounded with a sleep.

Act 4, Scene 1

The drama of Shakespeare

When people go to the theatre and see a Shakespeare play, or read his plays in a book, they quite often find themselves wondering what makes it all so special.

I'd say it's not for one reason alone, but for a whole set of reasons. In this section, I'm going to look at one scene from one play and see how Shakespeare is able to draw us in and make us feel all sorts of different and powerful emotions. I'll be looking at the way he tells a story, fills the scene with images and shows us how people think.

Romeo and Juliet

In the play *Romeo and Juliet*, one of the scenes shows us a father yelling at his daughter. These are some of the things he calls her: "young baggage", "disobedient wretch", "you green-sickness carrion", "you tallow-face, wretched puling fool", "whining maumet" (puppet).

Young baggage, disobedient wretch, whining maumet.
Mum! He called me a whining maumet.
Oh, did he, dear?

Many of us know what it feels like to get into a row with our parents. Parents tell a young person to do something and the young person says no. Juliet, who's only thirteen, faces up to her father and dares to tell him that she doesn't want to marry Paris, the man her parents have chosen for her.

She doesn't tell her father that she has fallen in love with Romeo instead, and by now in the play we know that it would be the most dangerous thing she could do. That's because there is a terrible feud going on between Romeo's family and Juliet's family. What's more, all fighting has been banned by the city's ruler, on pain of death.

It gets worse! Romeo's best friend has just been killed by Juliet's cousin, Tybalt, in a street gangfight. In revenge, Romeo kills

Tybalt. In the midst of all this murder and danger, Juliet is daring to go against her father's wishes. She has married Romeo in secret, even though he's from the enemy family and he's murdered one of her close relatives!

When Juliet's father first appears in the scene, Juliet is crying and he talks to her with kind words. He conjures up a picture for Juliet of herself, describing her crying as if her body were a boat sailing on a sea of tears, blown by a wind of sighs:

> **...The barque* thy body is,**
> **Sailing in this salt flood; the wind thy sighs,**
> **Who, raging with thy tears and they with them,**
> **Without a sudden calm will overset**
> **Thy tempest-tossèd body.**
> *Act 3, Scene 5*

***barque** boat

But a moment later, this tender feeling is shattered and he is plunged into a rage with her. He hears from his wife that Juliet doesn't want to marry Paris, and worse, Juliet infuriates him by answering back, playing with his words: "proud" and "thanks". You can almost hear him gasping for breath as he shouts:

> **How, how, how, how – chopped logic?**
> *Act 3, Scene 5*

And in his fury, Shakespeare has him twisting the grammar of the English language:

> **Thank me no thankings, nor proud me no prouds...**
> *Act 3, Scene 5*

just as a parent today might say, "Don't you

'that's rubbish' me!"

As we've already heard, he shouts abuse at her:

Hang thee, young baggage, disobedient wretch!
Act 3, Scene 5

And finally he threatens to throw her out of the house:

Graze where you will, you shall not house
with me
...hang, beg, starve, die in the streets,
For, by my soul, I'll ne'er acknowledge thee...
Act 3, Scene 5

In this one scene we can see some of the amazing ways in which Shakespeare works. The tension and fear from the street violence and killings make everything that Juliet wants for herself appear incredibly risky and dangerous. There's a moment of hope and peace expressed in the beautiful, soothing poetry the father speaks to the daughter he loves. Then, when she defies him, Shakespeare's words show us great depth of feeling: the father's rage that his young daughter won't do what he wants. What's more, Shakespeare shows us a man so wound up with his own place in society that he cares about this more than his daughter's feelings:

> **Day, night; work, play;**
> **Alone, in company, still my care hath been**
> **To have her matched; and having now provided**
> **A gentleman of noble parentage...**
> *Act 3, Scene 5*

So he threatens her with financial ruin, utter destruction. And all the time this is going on, we know something that he doesn't: Juliet is married to Romeo, the son of his sworn enemy.

Earlier in the play, Shakespeare uses what's known as the soliloquy to show us how Juliet feels. This is when he gives a window into his characters' minds and lets us hear what they are thinking. In real life, people don't often make speeches out loud when they're on their own, but in Shakespeare's plays we find ourselves listening to these speeches and what they tell us about the workings of the human mind.

Here's Juliet, in an earlier scene, talking to herself and us:

Come night, come Romeo; come, thou day in night,

For thou wilt lie upon the wings of night
Whiter than new snow on a raven's back.
Come, gentle night; come, loving, black-browed
night,
Give me my Romeo, and when I shall die
Take him and cut him out in little stars,
And he will make the face of heaven so fine
That all the world will be in love with night
And pay no worship to the garish sun.
Act 3, Scene 2

We can read these words on the page and admire them, but we also have to remember Shakespeare wrote them in a play – something performed to a live audience. And by the time the audience watch the scene where Juliet and her parents are arguing, it can feel almost unbearable because of what they already know. Only the kindness of Juliet's nanny, the Nurse, relieves the situation. And the argument ends with the chill horror of Juliet's mother turning on her daughter:

> **Talk not to me, for I'll not speak a word.**
> **Do as thou wilt, for I have done with thee.**
> *Act 3, Scene 5*

So in this scene we can see some of the ways Shakespeare makes his plays so special. He does it through the action, that is, what people do – things like Juliet's mother and father being angry with their daughter, or Juliet falling in love with Romeo. He does it through how the characters spark off each other, each picking up on what the other says – we see this when Juliet and her father use their words against each other. He does it through the tension we feel when we know more of what's going on than the character who is speaking – we see this when we know what Juliet has done, even though her mother and father don't. And he does it through the pictures in the words the characters speak – we see this with the boat sailing on a sea of tears at the beginning of the scene. Indeed, his plays are full of this kind of pictorial language. Such writing was extraordinary four hundred years ago and it is still extraordinary.

The will

Apart from poems and plays, we know of one other thing that Shakespeare wrote: his will. People have pored over it for centuries trying to figure out what he really meant.

The phrase that amuses many people is where he says that he will leave his wife his "second best bed". "Why didn't he leave her his best bed?" they ask. Perhaps he didn't love her? Perhaps she knew that she was going to get the best bed, but he was simply saying she could have the second best as well? Historians have argued over these words. Some say that his wife would have got one third of all Shakespeare's Stratford houses and land anyway – the "widow's dower". Not so, say recent historians. In that part of the country, widows didn't have this right. So maybe Shakespeare's wife did only get his second-best bed and had to rely on the goodwill of her family and friends to support her for the rest of her life.

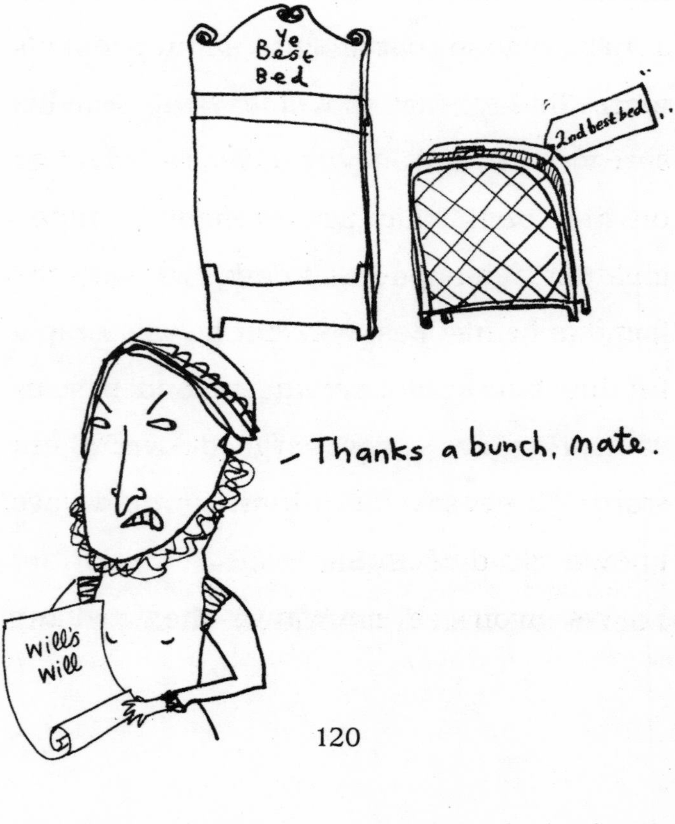

Whatever the truth is, we can definitely say that, in his will, Shakespeare left more of what he owned to one daughter, Susanna, than to the other, Judith. Susanna could read and was married to a doctor, while Judith couldn't read and had just married someone who was known in Stratford to be a rather dodgy, unfaithful fellow. What's more, Shakespeare rewrote his will to make sure that his property and wealth would go on being passed down through Susanna's children. When you match this up with the fact that he had helped create a coat of arms for his family, you build up a picture of someone who was very interested in starting a new, well-off family line – what's known as a dynasty.

We won't ever know whether any

character in a Shakespeare play is saying something that Shakespeare thought about his own life, but in King Lear he shows us an old man struggling with how to share out his wealth amongst his children. Perhaps, and we can only ever say "perhaps", Shakespeare spent some time in his life worrying about who to leave his money to. Perhaps, like King Lear, he also worried about whether leaving more money to one child than another was to do with whether you love one child more than another. When King Lear finally comes to see that Cordelia, the daughter he rejected, really loved him, he has been driven mad, but in his madness he has a vision and he says to her:

Come, let's away to prison.
We two alone will sing like birds i'th' cage.
When thou dost ask me blessing, I'll kneel down
And ask of thee forgiveness; so we'll live,
And pray, and sing, and tell old tales, and laugh
At gilded butterflies...
King Lear*, *Act 5, Scene 3

When all is said, we know next to nothing about what made Shakespeare happy, angry or sad. In other words, we don't know anything about his emotional life. But through the documents that have survived, we do have a very clear picture of someone who started out as the son of a small tradesman and ended up as a wealthy landowner. He was also, of course, the most famous writer of his time.

Shakespeare died on 23 April 1616, around his fifty-second birthday. On his tomb is written:

> **Good friend, for Jesu's sake forbear**
> **To dig the dust enclosed here.**
> **Blest be the man that spares these stones**
> **And cursed be he that moves my bones.**

Quite why there is such a threat, no one knows.

The legacy

Do you ever say that someone is "tongue-tied" or that something is as "dull as ditchwater"? Have you ever said that someone "wouldn't budge an inch"? Have you ever heard someone say that he or she "has seen better days"? Perhaps you've heard people say he's his "own flesh and blood", it "set your teeth on edge", that the "game is up", it's "without rhyme or reason", it happened in "one fell swoop", it "melted into thin air", "that's the long and short of it" and "the truth will out".

If you've used or heard any of these expressions then that was Shakespeare talking. Some words we use every day first appeared in his writing, and were perhaps invented by him: "hint", "leap-frog", "lonely", "excellent" and "gloomy" are just some of them. But it's not only his words and expressions that have lasted. Every day of every year someone somewhere in the world is reading Shakespeare, and people are acting in his plays and watching them. Somewhere someone like me is writing a book about his writing.

What all this means is that Shakespeare's writing is part of world culture. His words are so familiar that, when people try to understand something, or imagine something, or describe it, their minds turn to a scene or character from Shakespeare.

Everyone comes to Shakespeare's writing for different reasons and takes different things from it. When people are feeling tired or fed up they sometimes think of the murdering king Macbeth, in despair of his life, seeing time passing as a terrible burden:

> **Tomorrow, and tomorrow, and tomorrow**
> **Creeps in this petty pace from day to day**
> **To the last syllable of recorded time...**
> ***Macbeth***, *Act 5, Scene 5*

Some people enjoy Shakespeare's colourful insults: "Pernicious blood-sucker of sleeping men" ... "long-tongued, babbling gossip" ... "smiling, smooth, detested parasites" ... "loathsomest scab in Greece".

Some people like using little phrases from Shakespeare as a way of answering or interrupting. They might say: "But me no buts" when they want someone to stop giving excuses; "Parting is such sweet sorrow" when saying goodbye; "Why, this is very midsummer madness" when crazy things are going on; "The lady protests too much, methinks" when they suspect someone who's overreacting is probably guilty; "All that glisters is not gold" to mean something may not be as good as it looks.

Sometimes it's the jokes people remember. In *Twelfth Night*, for instance, a noblewoman calls to her servants to get rid of the jester: "Take the fool away", and the jester comes in with, "Do you not hear, fellows? Take away the lady". And in *Much Ado About Nothing*, Shakespeare pokes fun at the way an ordinary policeman gets all mixed up when he tries to use posh legal language. He says:

> **Our watch,* sir, have indeed comprehended two auspicious persons...**
> ***Much Ado About Nothing***, *Act 3, Scene 5*

***watch** police

instead of "apprehended two suspicious persons". Later, he says:

> **Marry, sir, they have committed false report, moreover they have spoken untruths, secondarily they are slanders, sixth and lastly they have belied a lady, thirdly they have verified unjust things, and to conclude, they are lying knaves.**
>
> ***Much Ado About Nothing**, Act 5, Scene 1*

So the policeman ends up saying the same thing in six different ways. Not that he can count either!

For over three hundred years after Shakespeare's death, we find that people didn't always perform the whole of his plays and that sometimes they rewrote them. There was even a time when actors used to put shows together of what they thought were the great speeches.

In the last hundred years there have been other changes. The plays have been put on in modern dress, as operas, musicals, ballets and films.

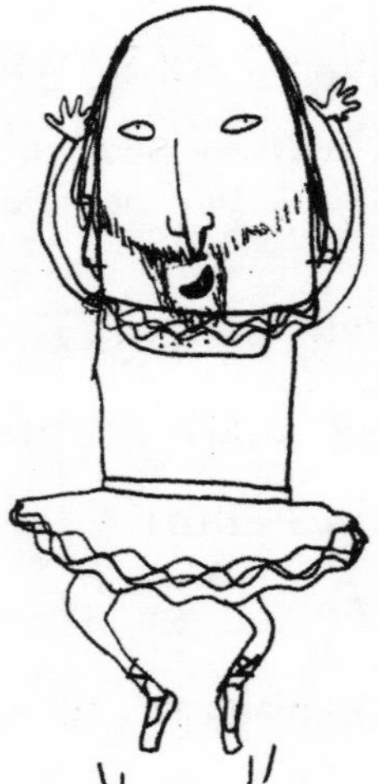

Some of these cut and change the original scripts. Perhaps the most famous and striking has been *Romeo and Juliet*, starring Leonardo DiCaprio and Claire Danes. Using only Shakespeare's words, but cut down by well over two thirds of the play, the film is set in modern America, backed by rock music. Some people thought that it wrecked Shakespeare, but others thought that it was one of the best ever ways to keep Shakespeare alive.

If any part of this book has grabbed your attention, if there's anything about Shakespeare and what he wrote that has made you stop and wonder, then don't leave it at that. You could hire a video of one of the Shakespeare films. Perhaps a theatre near you is putting on one of the plays. Why not go? But before you do, you could find one of those books that tell the story of the play. If you read it before you go, it might help you to concentrate. If you're studying Shakespeare at school, it's great to get a chance to act out some of it – even just one short scene. Then you see that Shakespeare didn't really write books, he wrote scripts – scenes and speeches for people to say out loud and act out in front of other people.

Shakespeare himself knew just how powerful this can be. In *Hamlet*, Prince Hamlet arranges for a group of travelling players to put on a play that acts out the murder of his father. It is performed in front of Claudius, the new king, the one who actually did the murder. At the moment when the play shows a man poisoning a king, just as Claudius has murdered Hamlet's father, the real Claudius can't bear it any longer and rushes out shouting, "Give me some light!"

Yes, watching a play – watching a Shakespeare play – can be that striking. Try it.

Timeline

Shakespeare's age appears after the date. The dates for his plays are what scholars suggest. They are not certain or definite.

1557

- England begins a two-year war with France.

1558

- Elizabeth, daughter of Henry VIII and Anne Boleyn, becomes Queen of England.
- Explorer Anthony Jenkinson travels round Russia.

1560

- The Geneva Bible – an early version of the Bible in English – is published.

1561

- The first play to be written in the same rhythm as Shakespeare's plays – blank verse – is performed in London (*Gorboduc* by T. Norton and T. Sackville).

1562

- John Hawkins is the first Englishman to trade in slaves, taking them from Sierra Leone in Africa to Hispaniola (now Cuba) in the Caribbean.

1563

- Twenty thousand people die of the plague in London.

1564

William Shakespeare is born in Henley Street, Stratford-upon-Avon, son of John and Mary, on or

around 23rd April.
• Two hundred people die of the plague in Stratford.
• Work starts on building Britain's first canal.

1567

Three years old.
• London's first purpose-built theatre is made at the Red Lion, Whitechapel.
• James Stuart is crowned James VI of Scotland at one year old.

1568

Four years old.
• The Geneva Bible is revised and published as the Bishops' Bible. Shakespeare would have read both versions.

1569

Five years old.
• Elizabeth I crushes the Revolt of the Northern Earls, a Roman Catholic uprising in the north of England.

1570

Six years old.
Shakespeare's father is found guilty of usury – making too much profit from lending money.
• Pope Pius V excommunicates Elizabeth I – that means she is forbidden to be part of the Roman Catholic Church.

1571

Seven years old.
• The Ridolfi Plot against the Queen.
• A law is passed saying that a person found doing something under instruction from the Pope will be charged with treason and, if found guilty, will be executed.

1576

Twelve years old.
John Shakespeare, William's father, is almost completely broke.
• Travelling players –

Leicester's Men and Worcester's Men – visit Stratford.
• The Theatre, a theatre that William Shakespeare will use, opens in Shoreditch, London.
• Vagrants (unemployed people on the move) are forced to go to Bridewell, a kind of prison.
• Explorer Martin Frobisher travels in what is now northern Canada.

1577

Thirteen years old.
• The Curtain Theatre in Shoreditch opens.
• Francis Drake leaves Plymouth to sail around the world.

1579

Fifteen years old.
• Travelling players – Lord Strange's Men and the Countess of Essex's Men – visit Stratford.
• *The School of Abuse*, a pamphlet attacking plays and poetry, is published.
• A rebellion in Ireland is ruthlessly put down by English troops.
• Francis Drake lands just north of what is now San Francisco and declares it New Albion, part of England.

1580

Sixteen years old.
• Nine Roman Catholics land in Dover with the aim of overthrowing the Queen. The Roman Catholic Church promises that the assassination of Queen Elizabeth would be "a glorious work" and not a sin.

1581

Seventeen years old.
• To convert to being a Roman Catholic is now treason. A person can be sentenced to death for it.

1582

Eighteen years old.
Shakespeare marries Anne Hathaway.

1583

Nineteen years old.
Susanna, William and Anne's first child, is baptized.
• *The Anatomy of Abuses*, a pamphlet attacking plays and players, is published.
• The Throckmorton Plot to kill the Queen. The Spanish ambassador is involved.
• Explorer Humphrey Gilbert starts a settlement in Newfoundland, now in Canada.

1585

Twenty-one years old.
Hamnet and Judith, William and Anne's twins, are baptized.
• A Member of Parliament is executed for threatening to kill the Queen.
• England is at war with Spain, and English troops are sent to Holland.

1586

Twenty-two years old.
• The Babington Plot against Elizabeth. Her cousin, Mary, Queen of Scots, is accused of being part of it.
• As a way of trying to control Puritans, a law is passed saying that all pamphlets on religion must be approved by the Church.
• The first potatoes are brought to Britain from Colombia.

1587

Twenty-three years old.
Shakespeare probably arrives in London around this time.
• The Rose Theatre opens on Bankside, Southwark, near the present new Globe Theatre.
• Christopher Marlowe's

spectacular play *Tamburlaine the Great* and Thomas Kyd's *The Spanish Tragedy* are written around this time.

- Elizabeth I orders the execution of her cousin Mary, Queen of Scots, for being involved with the Babington Plot.
- A Member of Parliament, Peter Wentworth, is imprisoned for asking for more freedom of speech.

1588

Twenty-four years old.

- Drama, new plays and productions in London's theatres start to happen from now on.
- A Catholic priest is executed in public close to the Theatre.
- The Spanish Armada is defeated off the coast of England.

(1589–91)
Shakespeare writes
• Henry VI
(in three parts)

1591

Twenty-seven years old.

- The Queen's favourite, the Earl of Essex, is in France helping Protestants to fight Roman Catholics.
- Explorer James Lancaster leaves for the East Indies (now Indonesia).

1592

Twenty-eight years old.
Shakespeare's play Henry VI is performed at the Rose Theatre.

- Robert Greene writes his attack on Shakespeare, calling him an "upstart crow" (*see* page 41).
- London theatres are officially closed due to riots by apprentices.
- London clothing workers in Southwark (near where the Globe Theatre will be) riot against changes in the industry and the arrival of foreign workers from France and Holland.
- A midsummer street festival near Bankside

ends in bloodshed as the authorities kill "several innocent persons".

• Severe plague in London for two years. The theatres are closed.

• Spanish treasure is seized by English ships.

(1592–3)
Shakespeare writes
• Richard III
• Titus Andronicus
• Venus and Adonis

1593

Twenty-nine years old.

Shakespeare's long poem *Venus and Adonis* is entered in the Stationers' Register. This gave a book-seller the licence to print and publish it as a book.

• Playwright Christopher Marlowe is stabbed to death in a tavern brawl.

• Five Puritans are executed for not accepting the Queen's right to rule the Church.

• Eleven thousand people die of the plague in London.

(1593–4)
Shakespeare writes
• The Comedy of Errors
• The Taming of the Shrew
• The Rape of Lucrece

1594

Thirty years old.

***The Comedy of Errors* is performed at Gray's Inn in London.**

Shakespeare's long poem *The Rape of Lucrece* is entered in the Stationers' Register.

Shakespeare is listed as one of the Lord Chamberlain's Men.

• Bad harvests in England mean high prices and starvation.

• The Queen's doctor, a Portuguese Jew, is accused of trying to poison her and is executed.

• English troops are sent to put down an uprising by Roman Catholics in Ireland.

(1594–5)
Shakespeare writes
- **The Two Gentlemen of Verona**
- **Love's Labour's Lost**

1595

Thirty-one years old.
- Theatres in London are officially closed for two months after riots over food prices.
- It is said by the London authorities that "disorderly people of the common sort ... assemble themselves" and do "ungodly" things at holiday time, and "apprentices and servants" catch plague from the new playhouses.
- Famous Roman Catholic priest and poet, Robert Southwell, is tortured and executed for treason.
- Spain raids Cornish seaside towns of Penzance and Mousehole.
- England is at war with Ireland.
- Explorer Sir Walter Raleigh is in the north-east part of Latin America, what is now Venezuela

(1595–6)
Shakespeare writes
- **Romeo and Juliet**
- **Richard II**
- **A Midsummer Night's Dream**

1596

Thirty-two years old.
Shakespeare's eleven-year-old son Hamnet dies.
- There are riots and rebellions in Oxfordshire and the Midlands against "gentlemen", enclosures, poverty and hunger.
- It is warned in a message to the Queen's adviser that this year "will be the hardest year for the poor in man's memory" and that as a result "there would be cutting of throats".
- The first water-flushing toilet is installed in the Queen's palace in Richmond.

(1596–7)
Shakespeare writes
- **King John**
- **The Merchant of Venice**

1597

Thirty-three years old.
Shakespeare buys New Place, a house in Stratford.
Shakespeare is reported for not paying taxes in St Helen's parish, Bishopsgate, London.
- The top court in the land hears petition from London authorities to ban all stage plays.
- Famine in and near Stratford is at its worst this winter.

(1597–8)
Shakespeare writes
- **Henry IV (both parts)**

1598

Thirty-four years old.
The Theatre is dismantled by Shakespeare's company (*see* pages 9–12).
For the first time, a play is published under Shakespeare's name: *Love's Labour's Lost*.
Shakespeare acts in *Every Man in his Humour*, a play by Ben Jonson.
Shakespeare is found to be hoarding grain, hoping that prices might rise.
Shakespeare invests in "knitted stockings".
- Opening of the first workhouses – places where unemployed people are sent to live.
- English troops are defeated in Ireland.

(1598–9)
Shakespeare writes
- **Much Ado About Nothing**
- **Henry V**
- **The Merry Wives of Windsor**

1599

Thirty-five years old.
The Globe Theatre is built

and opened on Bankside, Southwark. Shakespeare and other members of the Lord Chamberlain's Men own shares in it. *Julius Caesar* may have been one of the first plays to be performed there. Shakespeare is reported for not paying his taxes.

(1599–1600)
Shakespeare writes
- **Julius Caesar**
- **As You Like It**
- **Twelfth Night**

1600

Thirty-six years old.
Henry IV is performed at Court.
- There is bitter war and starvation in Ireland. Many royal woods are cut down to pay for it.
- The telescope is invented in Holland.

(1600–1)
Shakespeare writes
- **Hamlet**
- **Troilus and Cressida**

1601

Thirty-seven years old.
Shakespeare's father dies. By special request from the Earl of Essex's supporters, *Richard II* (including some lines that the Queen might have thought were treasonable) is performed at the Globe Theatre the day before Essex's rebellion. Essex is later beheaded.
- Three thousand Spanish troops land in Ireland to fight the English.

1602

Thirty-eight years old.
Shakespeare buys several pieces of land and a cottage in Stratford.

(1602–3)
Shakespeare writes
- **All's Well That Ends Well**
- **Othello**

1603

Thirty-nine years old.
The Lord Chamberlain's Men become the King's Men with Shakespeare a prominent member.
• Elizabeth I dies and James VI of Scotland is crowned James I of England.
• A petition is presented to the King with one thousand signatures from Puritans asking to abolish "ritual" in church services.
• Thirty thousand people die of the plague in London. The theatres are closed.
• Rebellion in Ireland is defeated by English troops.
• The first English bank is set up.

(1603–4)
Shakespeare writes
• Measure for Measure

1604

Forty years old.
• Peace with Spain.

(1604–5)
Shakespeare writes
• Timon of Athens

1605

Forty-one years old.
Shakespeare buys the right to collect taxes (tithes) from some people living near Stratford. ***Henry V*** **and** ***The Merchant of Venice*** **are performed at court.**
• Guy Fawkes and others try to blow up the Houses of Parliament in the Gunpowder Plot.

(1605–6)
Shakespeare writes
• Macbeth
• King Lear

1606

Forty-two years old.
• A law is passed saying that Roman Catholics cannot hold public office.
• Portuguese explorers reach seas north of Australia.

(1606–7)
Shakespeare writes
• Antony and Cleopatra

1607

Forty-three years old.
Shakespeare's daughter Susanna marries Dr John Hall in Stratford. Shakespeare's brother Edmund dies.
• Riots against common land being enclosed in Northamptonshire and Leicestershire.
• Flight of the northern earls from Ireland.
• Settlement of Virginia (now in the USA).

(1607–8)
Shakespeare writes
• Coriolanus

1608

Forty-four years old.
Shakespeare's grand-daughter Elizabeth is born. Shakespeare's mother dies.

(1608–9)
Shakespeare writes
• Pericles

1609

Forty-five years old.
Shakespeare's *Sonnets* are published.
• English and Scots Protestants start settling in great numbers in northern part of Ireland.
• Tea arrives in Europe from China.

(1609–10)
Shakespeare writes
• Cymbeline

1610

Forty-six years old.
Shakespeare returns to live in Stratford.
• First use of the fork in England, introduced from Italy.

(1610–11)
Shakespeare writes
• The Winter's Tale

1611

Forty-seven years old.
The Winter's Tale **is put on at court.**
• The best-known and most popular edition of the Bible, the Authorized Version, is published.
• House of Commons attacks some of the King's rights to rule.

(1611–12)
Shakespeare writes
• The Tempest

1612

Forty-eight years old.
Shakespeare's brother Gilbert dies.
• "Jigs, Rhymes and Dances after Plays" are banned to prevent "tumults" in the streets of London.

(1612-13)
Shakespeare, possibly with John Fletcher, writes
• Henry VIII

1613

Forty-nine years old.
Shakespeare's brother Richard dies.
Shakespeare buys a building in Blackfriars, London.
The Globe Theatre burns down.
Shakespeare's company puts on several plays at court during festivities for the wedding of James I's daughter Elizabeth.

(1613–14)
Shakespeare, possibly with John Fletcher, writes
• The Two Noble Kinsmen

1614

Fifty years old.
The rebuilt Globe Theatre opens.
Shakespeare and his son-in-law, Dr John Hall, are

in London on business over tithes.

• House of Commons tries to stop the King raising money in whatever ways he wants.

1615

Fifty-one years old.
Shakespeare is named in the dispute and rebellion over land enclosures near Stratford.

• Seventeen convicts are saved from hanging on condition they be transported to Virginia.

1616

Fifty-two years old.
Shakespeare's daughter Judith marries Thomas Quiney in Stratford. Not long afterwards he is tried for making another woman pregnant. Shakespeare writes and rewrites his will (*see* pages 119–123). He dies on 23rd April and is buried in Stratford two days later.

1623

Shakespeare's wife Anne dies.
The first major collection of Shakespeare's plays, *The First Folio*, is published.

Index

G

H

I

J

K

L

T

W

Bibliography

◆ ***William Shakespeare: The Complete Works***
ed. Stanley Wells and Gary Taylor
(Oxford, Clarendon Press, 1988)

◆ **Baird, David**
Shakespeare at the Globe
(London, MQ Publications Ltd, 1998)

◆ **Chute, Marchette**
Shakespeare of London
(New York, E.P. Dutton, 1949)

◆ **Claybourne, Anna and Treays, Rebecca**
The World of Shakespeare
(London, Usborne Publishing, 1996)

◆ **Garfield, Leon**
Shakespeare Stories
(London, Victor Gollancz Ltd, 1985)

◆ **Greenhill, Wendy**
Shakespeare's Theatre
(Oxford, Heinemann, 1995)

◆ **Greenhill, Wendy and Wignall, Paul**
Shakespeare: A Life
(Oxford, Heinemann, 1996)

◆ **Greenhill, Wendy and Wignall, Paul**
Shakespeare's Players
(Oxford, Heinemann, 1996)

◆ **Greenhill, Wendy and Wignall, Paul**
Shakespeare, Man of the Theatre
(Oxford, Heinemann Library, 1999)

◆ **Grun, Bernard**
The Timetables of History
(New York, Simon & Schuster, 1982)

◆ **Halliday, F.E.**
A Shakespeare Companion
(London, Penguin Books Ltd, 1964)

◆ **Hill, Wayne F. and Ottchen, Cynthia J.**
Shakespeare's Insults, Educating Your Wit
(London, Vermilion, 1991)

◆ **Holden, Anthony**
William Shakespeare
(London, Little, Brown and Company, 1999)

◆ **Honan, Park**
Shakespeare: A Life
(Oxford, Oxford University Press, 1999)

◆ **Laroque, Francois**
Shakespeare: Court, Crowd and Playhouse
(London, Thames and Hudson Ltd, 1993)

◆ **Manley, Lawrence (ed.)**
London in the Age of Shakespeare: An Anthology
(London, Croom Helm, 1986)

◆ **Morgan, Kenneth O. (ed.)**
The Oxford History of Britain
(Oxford, Oxford University Press, 1988)

◆ **Palmer, Alan and Veronica**
The Chronology of British History – From 250,000 BC to Present Day
(London, Century, 1992)

◆ **Thomson, Peter**
Shakespeare's Professional Career
(Cambridge, Cambridge University Press, 1992)

◆ **Toropov, Brandon**
Shakespeare for Beginners
(London, Writers and Readers, 1997)

◆ **Weinstein, Rosemary**
Tudor London
(London, HMSO, 1994)

◆ **Wells, Stanley**
Shakespeare: A Life in Drama
(London, W.W. Norton and Co., 1995)

◆ **Williams, E.N.**
The Penguin Dictionary of English and European History 1485–1789
(London, Penguin Books Ltd, 1980)

◆ **Wilson, Richard**
Will Power: Essays on Shakespearean Authority
(London, Harvester Wheatsheaf, 1993)

PLAY

Will

At this very moment, someone, somewhere in the world, is reading Shakespeare. And, though he died nearly 400 years ago, someone else is writing about him, or acting in one of his plays.

Find out what makes Shakespeare so special in Michael Rosen's brilliant introduction to his work and world.

"Rosen has the rare gift of being able to talk plainly and engagingly to children about sophisticated ideas."
The Sunday Times

Another title in this series
What's so special about Dickens?

www.walker.co.uk

ISBN 978-1-4063-6741-6

90100 >

9 781406 367416

£6.99 UK ONLY **eBook** available